THE ULTIMATE
LIVERPOOL F.C.
TRIVIA BOOK

A Collection of Amazing Trivia Quizzes
and Fun Facts for Die-Hard Liverpool Fans!

Ray Walker

Exclusive Free Book
Crazy Sports Stories

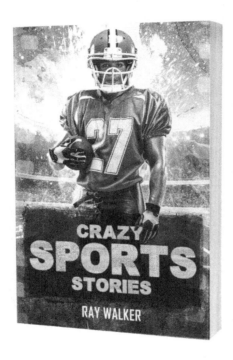

As a thank you for getting a copy of this book I would like to offer you a free copy of my book Crazy Sports Stories which comes packed with interesting stories from your favorite sports such as Football, Hockey, Baseball, Basketball and more.

**Grab your free copy over at
<u>RayWalkerMedia.com/Bonus</u>**

CONTENTS

INTRODUCTION

Known simply as "The Reds" by supporters across the globe, Liverpool F.C. is one of the most successful and beloved football clubs in the history of the sport.

The club's roots can actually be traced back to 1892, when John Houlding severed ties with local neighbors Everton F.C. and moved to the famous Anfield ground.

From that day forward, the club has left its footprint in football history by being crowned the kings of Europe six times and capturing 19 top-flight English championships as well as a record eight English League Cups.

There have been some lean times and unfortunate tragedy along the way at Heysel and Hillsborough, but their Premier League title drought finally came to an end in 2019-20, when they captured the championship in record-setting style.

Anfield has been home to many of the world's biggest stars over the years, such as Roger Hunt, Ian Callaghan, Ian Rush, Michael Owen, Ray Clemence, Kevin Keegan, Kenny Dalglish, Steven Gerrard, Luis Suárez, and Mohamed Salah. And who can forget legendary managers such as Bob Paisley and Bill Shankly.

It's no secret Liverpool attracts some of the most vociferous, passionate, loyal, and witty fans on the planet, as described in their famous theme song, "You'll Never Walk Alone."

The Liverpool F.C. trivia/fact book you have in front of you is filled with a wide variety of facts regarding the club from its humble beginnings to the beginning of the 2020-21 football campaign.

It includes 12 unique sections, with each one containing a specific quiz. Every chapter is designed to test your overall knowledge about the club and comes with 20 brain-teasers that offer multiple-choice and true-false questions, with the answers revealed on a later page. Each of the dozen chapters also contains 10 historical "Did You Know?" anecdotes concerning Liverpool's history, players, and managers, etc.

The team's supporters can take a quick history lesson with the book, as well as re-live the ups and downs the club has enjoyed and endured for well over a century. You might even be able to gather some new tidbits of information along the way, and it's the perfect tool to help you arm yourself with as much knowledge as possible before your next quiz and trivia challenge come a knocking.

Liverpool fans will hopefully enjoy this historical scrapbook and feel loud and proud about the club's incredible achievements.

CHAPTER 1:

ORIGINS & HISTORY

QUIZ TIME!

1. What year was Liverpool F.C. founded?

    a. 1895
    b. 1892
    c. 1890
    d. 1893

2. Which league did the newly formed club play their first competitive season in?

    a. Football Alliance
    b. The Combination
    c. Football League
    d. Lancashire League

3. The club was originally known as Everton Athletic.

    a. True
    b. False

4. Who was the founder of Liverpool F.C.?

    a. John McKenna
    b. Alex Raisbeck
    c. John Houlding
    d. Bill Shankly

5. Liverpool's first-ever recorded game was a friendly game against which club?

    a. Preston North End
    b. Higher Walton
    c. Blackpool F.C
    d. Rotherham Town

6. What was the final score of the club's first match and victory in the Lancashire League?

    a. 2-2
    b. 8-0
    c. 3-1
    d. 4-0

7. Liverpool finished their only season in the Lancashire League in what place?

    a. 5th
    b. 1st
    c. 7th
    d. 3rd

8. Anfield Stadium has been the home of Liverpool ever since the club's inception.

    a. True
    b. False

4

9. How many matches did Liverpool win in the Lancashire League?

    a. 15
    b. 16
    c. 17
    d. 18

10. In the club's first year in the Second Division, how many points did they total?

    a. 50
    b. 36
    c. 33
    d. 46

11. Liverpool won 12 matches and avoided relegation to the Second Division in 1894-95.

    a. True
    b. False

12. How many times have Liverpool been relegated to the Second Division as of 2020?

    a. 2
    b. 4
    c. 3
    d. 5

13. Liverpool scored how many goals in their first campaign in the First Division.

    a. 106
    b. 51

c. 77

d. 46

14. In the club's first season in the Premier League, they drew 15 matches.

    a. True

    b. False

15. What was the final score of Liverpool's first friendly match victory in 1892?

    a. 2-1

    b. 6-4

    c. 3-2

    d. 7-1

16. How any goals did Liverpool score in their first Premier League season?

    a. 58

    b. 53

    c. 47

    d. 62

17. Who was Liverpool's first fixture against in the Lancashire League?

    a. New Brighton Tower

    b. Fairfield Athletic

    c. Higher Walton

    d. Bury F.C.

18. What was the result of the club's first Premier League match?

a. Loss

b. Win

c. Draw

d. 2-1 Win

19. Which club did Liverpool play in their first Premier League match?

   a. Leeds United

   b. Arsenal

   c. Sheffield United

   d. Nottingham Forrest

20. The Football League denied Liverpool's first application to join the league.

   a. True

   b. False

QUIZ ANSWERS

1. B – 1892

2. D – Lancashire League

3. A – True

4. C – John Houlding

5. D – Rotherham Town

6. B – 8-0

7. B – 1st

8. A – True

9. C – 17

10. A – 50

11. B – False

12. C – 3

13. B – 51

14. B – False

15. D – 7-1

16. D – 62

17. C – Higher Walton

18. A – 0-1 Loss

19. D – Nottingham Forrest

20. A – True

DID YOU KNOW?

1. Liverpool Football Club (F.C.) of the English Premier League was originally founded in 1892 when John Houlding left the board of Everton F.C. in Liverpool to form a new club. The team, which is nicknamed "The Reds," plays in the city of Liverpool, Merseyside, Lancashire, with Anfield Stadium being its home ground. Their first recorded competitive contest was an 8-0 victory over a club known as Higher Walton on September 3, 1892. However, they also beat Rotherham Town 7-1 in a friendly outing just two days earlier.

2. John Houlding was originally on the board of Everton F.C., which was founded in 1878 and was a founding member of the Football League in 1888. He rented the pitch at Anfield to Everton for the club's home games, but Everton left the ground in 1892 and relocated at Goodison Park. Houlding now had a ground but no team to play in it, so he decided to form a new club which eventually became Liverpool F.C.

3. Liverpool F.C. was originally named Everton F.C. and Athletic Grounds Ltd. and was simply known as Everton Athletic. However, the Football Association refused to recognize the name since it was too similar to Everton F.C. Liverpool played in the local Lancashire League in 1892-93 and were crowned league champions at the end of the

campaign. They were then admitted to the Second Division of the Football League in 1893-94 season.

4. Liverpool won the Second Division in their first season in the Football League in 1893-94 by going unbeaten in 28 games, with 22 wins and 6 draws. They were then promoted to the First Division after winning a knockout match with Newton Heath, the last place team in the First Division. However, they were relegated back to the Second Division after just one season in the top flight when they won just seven of 30 contests and lost a knockout match against Bury, the top team in the Second Division.

5. Liverpool's first of 19 top-flight English league titles came in 1900-01 when they won the First Division, but they didn't win the FA Cup until 1964-65. Their first Football League Cup (EFL) was then won in 1980-81. Liverpool tasted European glory for the first time in 1972-73 when they won the UEFA Cup. Their first of six European Cup/Champions League triumphs took place in 1976-77, and they captured the FIFA World Club Cup for the first time in 2019.

6. The Anfield football ground was built and opened in 1884, with Everton using it as their home from 1884 until 1892 when Liverpool moved in. As of September 2020, Anfield's seating capacity was listed at 54,074, which made it England's seventh-largest football stadium. The record attendance at Anfield was 61,905, which was set during a

1952 game between Liverpool and Wolverhampton Wanderers in the fourth round of the FA Cup. The venue became an all-seating stadium in 1994, which reduced the capacity.

7. Liverpool has been owned by the Fenway Sports Group since October 2010, with Tom Werner being the current chairman. Fenway Sports Group was founded by John Henry and Werner and is a private entity which also owns the Boston Red Sox Major League Baseball (MLB) franchise as well as Anfield Stadium, Fenway Park in Boston, and numerous other subsidiaries. The company was originally known as New England Sports Ventures, with its name officially being changed in 2011. The group was formerly partnered with English football club Fulham F.C.

8. The club reached the FA Cup Final for the first time in 1913-14 but lost 1-0 to Burnley. They won league titles in 1922 and 1923, but didn't win any silverware again until the 1946-47 season when they topped the First Division. On April 24, 1954, The Reds were beaten 1-0 at home by Cardiff City and were relegated from the First Division to the Second. This meant almost 50 years of consecutive top-flight English football had come to an end. They didn't earn promotion back to the First Division until winning the Second Division Title in 1961-62.

9. For most of the club's history, the team's home colors have been all red. However, when Liverpool was founded, the

11

squad wore blue and white quartered shirts until 1894 when red shirts and white shorts were adopted. The club's badge originated in 1901 and features the liver bird, which is the city's symbol. The badge didn't show up on the kit until 1955 though. Liverpool changed to an all-red strip in 1964.

10. Former manager Bill Shankly felt an all-red strip of shirt, shorts, and socks would be a psychological benefit as the color represented power and danger. The team's away strip has typically been white or yellow shirts with black shorts. An all-gray kit was first used in 1987 and lasted until 1991-92 when it was replaced by green shirts and white shorts. Different color combinations were then used in the 1990s, and the gray kit came back in the 2008-09 season. There's also a third kit for European away matches and is used in domestic contests when the away kit clashes with the home team's kit.

CHAPTER 2:

THE CAPTAIN CLASS

QUIZ TIME!

1. How many recorded full-time captains has Liverpool had as of 2020?

    a. 28

    b. 60

    c. 41

    d. 33

2. Who was the club's first full-time captain born outside of the British Isles?

    a. Lucas Leiva

    b. Sami Hyypiä

    c. Dirk Kuyt

    d. Daniel Agger

3. Alex Raisbeck was the club's longest-serving captain.

    a. True

    b. False

4. Who was the first skipper of Liverpool?

    a. Harry Storer

    b. John McCartney

    c. Jimmy Ross

    d. Andrew Hannah

5. Which player served as captain from 1939 to 1940?

    a. Matt Busby

    b. Jimmy McInnes

    c. Bill Kinghorn

    d. Phil Taylor

6. Which player was captain in 1996-97?

    a. Paul Ince

    b. Ian Rush

    c. John Barnes

    d. Jamie Redknapp

7. Who was captain in 1988-89 and again in 1990-91?

    a. Mark Wright

    b. Steve Nicol

    c. Ronnie Whelan

    d. Phil Neal

8. Jordan Henderson has been the squad's captain since 2017.

    a. True

    b. False

9. Which season did Jamie Redknapp become skipper?

    a. 1997-98

    b. 1998-99

c. 1999-2000

d. 2000-01

10. How many years did Ron Yeats serve as The Reds' captain?

    a. 9

    b. 5

    c. 8

    d. 6

11. Mark Wright was the first captain of Liverpool in the Premier League era.

    a. True

    b. False

12. Who captained the club from 1979 to 1981?

    a. Howard Gayle

    b. Terry McDermott

    c. Phil Thompson

    d. Avi Cohen

13. Which player was captain between 1970 and 1973?

    a. Ron Yeats

    b. Tommy Smith

    c. Emlyn Hughes

    d. Dick White

14. Donald McKinlay served as captain for 11 seasons.

    a. True

    b. False

15. Which captain appeared in 210 matches for Liverpool?

    a. Ian Rush
    b. John Barnes
    c. Paul Ince
    d. Mark Wright

16. Who captained the club during their first top-flight league title win?

    a. Alex Raisbeck
    b. Harry Storer
    c. Arthur Goddard
    d. John McCartney

17. How many seasons was Graeme Souness the club's captain?

    a. 2
    b. 4
    c. 3
    d. 1

18. In 1955, Liverpool named which player the new captain?

    a. Dick White
    b. Eric Anderson
    c. Billy Liddell
    d. Jimmy Melia

19. Who was captain from 1913 to 1915?

    a. Tom Bromilow
    b. Donald McKinlay
    c. Ephraim Longworth
    d. Harry Lowe

20. Willie Fagan was full-time skipper between 1945 and 1947.

    a.   True

    b.   False

QUIZ ANSWERS

1. C – 41

2. B – Sami Hyypiä

3. B – False

4. D – Andrew Hannah

5. A – Matt Busby

6. C – John Barnes

7. C – Ronnie Whelan

8. B – False

9. C – 1999-2000

10. A – 9

11. A – True

12. C – Phil Thompson

13. B – Tommy Smith

14. B – False

15. D – Mark Wright

16. A – Alex Raisbeck

17. A – 2

18. C – Billy Liddell

19. D – Harry Lowe

20. A – True

DID YOU KNOW?

1. There has reportedly been 41 different full-time captains of The Reds since the club's inception. Andrew Hannah was the first to wear the armband in 1892, with Jordan Henderson being the latest since 2015 when Steven Gerrard departed the club. Ronnie Whelan was skipper in 1988-89 and again in 1990-91, with Alan Hansen occupying the position in between in 1989-90. Gerrard was also the longest-serving captain from 2003 to 2015.

2. Andrew Hannah, the squad's first skipper, held down the job from 1892 to 1895. The Scottish international right-back formerly played with Scottish side Renton and West Bromwich Albion and Everton in England before joining Liverpool. Hannah played with the club in the Lancashire League before the team entered the Football League. He was the first person to captain both Everton and Liverpool and helped the club win the Second Division title in 1893-94. It's believed he played 73 times for the club before departing in 1895.

3. As of 2020, Alex Raisbeck has been the second-longest serving skipper as he held the position from 1899 to 1909 as the side's fourth captain. The Scottish international defender turned pro at the age of 17, with Hibernian in his homeland, and also played with English outfit Stoke before joining The Reds in May 1898. He was appointed

captain at the age of 21 and skippered the team to its first top-flight league title in 1901. Raisbeck appeared in over 300 matches for Liverpool before going on to captain Partick Thistle in Scotland for five years starting 1899.

4. The first player to captain his club and country was English defender Ephraim Longworth. He signed with Liverpool in September 1910 and played more than 17 years with the club, with his last appearance coming in 1928 at the age of 40. He was first appointed captain in 1912-13 and was then handed the armband again for the 1920-21 campaign. He also skippered the English national side in 1921 in his second of five outings with his country. Longworth played in close to 400 contests with Liverpool and won a pair of top-flight league crowns.

5. Another player who reportedly enjoyed two stints as club captain was Scottish international left-back Donald McKinlay. He joined the team from Newton Villa in January 1910 and held the job in 1919-20 and again from 1921 to 1928, with the team winning the First Division title in 1921-22 and 1922-23. He left Liverpool in 1929 with 34 goals in 394 contests and ran a pub in the city after hanging up his boots.

6. Two Reds players with the last name Hughes have had the honor of being Liverpool captain. English international center-half Laurie Hughes played over 300 games with the team from 1943 to 1957 and was skipper in 1954-55. Emlyn Hughes was an English international defender/midfielder

who captained the side between 1973 and 1979. He played 665 times for the team and skippered it to four league titles and an FA Cup. He joined Liverpool in 1967 and also won two European and two UEFA Cup titles. He was also the Football Writers' Player of the Year for 1977 and had the honor of captaining England.

7. Sir Matt Busby became world famous as manager of Manchester United, but he played for archrivals Liverpool first and captained the team in 1939-40. The Scottish international attacker first played with Manchester City from 1928 to 1936 and played over 100 times for The Reds between 1936 and 1945. When Busby's playing days ended at Anfield, the club offered him an assistant coaching job. However, he wasn't satisfied with the amount of control over the squad he would be given and decided to join Man United instead. The rest, as they say, is history.

8. Between 1961 and 1970, Ron Yeats served as Liverpool captain. The Scottish international defender joined the club from Dundee United in Scotland and remained at Anfield until 1971, when he joined Tranmere Rovers. He played over 350 contests with Liverpool and captained the side to First Division titles in 1963-64 and 1965-66, as well as the 1964-65 FA Cup. After leaving The Reds, he served as player/manager with Tranmere Rovers and returned to Liverpool as a scout in 1986.

9. Former English international midfielder Jamie Redknapp comes from a famous footballing family as he's a cousin of

former midfielder Frank Lampard, the nephew of coach Frank Lampard Sr., and the son of former manager Harry Redknapp. Jamie joined Liverpool from Bournemouth and played 308 games with The Reds between 1991 and 2002 while serving as captain between 1999 and 2002. Redknapp became the youngest Liverpool player to compete in European competition in 1991.

10. A total of 15 full-time Liverpool captains have been Scottish, while 23 have hailed from England. There has also been one each from Wales (Ian Rush), the Republic of Ireland (Ronnie Whelan), and Finland (Sami Hyypiä). As of 2020, Hyypiä has been the only club captain born outside of the British Isles. Whelan was skipper in 1988-89 and 1990-91, while Rush held the title between 1993 and 1996, with Hyypiä wearing the armband between 2000 and 2003.

CHAPTER 3:

AMAZING MANAGERS

QUIZ TIME!

1. Who spent the most years as Liverpool's manager?

    a. Bill Shankly
    b. Bob Paisley
    c. Tom Watson
    d. George Patterson

2. What is former manager Kenny Dalglish's all-time win percentage?

    a. 60.63
    b. 58.26
    c. 54.25
    d. 57.57

3. From 1892 to 1896, the club had two acting managers.

    a. True
    b. False

4. Who served as the club's on-field manager from 1892 to 1896?

    a. John McKenna
    b. William Edward Barclay
    c. Tom Watson
    d. David Ashworth

5. What year was Jürgen Klopp named as Liverpool manager?

    a. 2014
    b. 2016
    c. 2015
    d. 2017

6. How many years did Tom Watson act as The Reds' boss?

    a. 20
    b. 18
    c. 15
    d. 19

7. Which manager has the lowest win percentage in club history?

    a. Graeme Souness
    b. Don Welsh
    c. Roy Evans
    d. Matt McQueen

8. As of 2020, Ronnie Moran is the only person who acted as a temporary caretaker manager.

    a. True
    b. False

9. Bill Shankly won how many games as Liverpool's manager?

    a. 407

    b. 329

    c. 402

    d. 358

10. How many matches did Joe Fagan manage for Liverpool?

    a. 164

    b. 139

    c. 150

    d. 131

11. Bill Shankly's squads conceded the most goals of any manager in the club's history.

    a. True

    b. False

12. How many matches did Tom Watson lose?

    a. 283

    b. 178

    c. 272

    d. 144

13. Who was the club's manager from 2012 to 2015?

    a. Rafael Benítez

    b. Kenny Dalglish

    c. Roy Hodgson

    d. Brendan Rogers

14. William Edward Barclay was the club's administrative manager from 1892 to 1896.

    a. True
    b. False

15. How many wins did Bob Paisley total in his managerial career with Liverpool?

    a. 310
    b. 299
    c. 308
    d. 305

16. How many full-time managers has Liverpool had as of 2020?

    a. 21
    b. 17
    c. 22
    d. 19

17. Which manager has the fourth-most draws in the club's history?

    a. George Kay
    b. Gérard Houllier
    c. George Patterson
    d. Rafael Benítez

18. How many matches did joint managers John McKenna and William Edward Barclay win in their 127 games?

    a. 65
    b. 76

c. 81

d. 77

19. Which manager has led Liverpool to the most trophies as of 2020?

   a. Bill Shankly

   b. Kenny Dalglish

   c. Bill Paisley

   d. Gérard Houllier

20. George Kay drew 100 contests as Liverpool's manager.

   a. True

   b. False

QUIZ ANSWERS

1. C – Tom Watson

2. B – 58.26

3. A – True

4. A – John McKenna

5. C – 2015

6. D – 19

7. B – Don Welsh

8. A – True

9. A – 407

10. D – 131

11. B – False

12. C – 272

13. D – Brendan Rogers

14. A – True

15. C – 308

16. A – 21

17. A – George Kay

18. D – 77

19. C – Bill Paisley

20. B – False

DID YOU KNOW?

1. There have been a total of 21 different, known full-time caretaker/managers for the club up until 2020, with Kenny Dalglish being the only person to manage the club on two different occasions. William Edward Barclay and John McKenna were considered to be co-managers from February 1892 to August 1896, as Barclay was known as the secretary-manager, while McKenna was considered to be the coach-manager.

2. Starting in August 1896, the rest of the club's managers have been Tom Watson, David Ashworth, Matt McQueen, George Patterson, George Kay, Don Welsh, Phil Taylor, Bill Shankly, Bob Paisley, Joe Fagan, Kenny Dalglish, Ronnie Moran, Graeme Souness, Roy Evans, Gerard Houllier, Rafael Benitez, Roy Hodgson, Kenny Dalglish again, and Brendan Rodgers. Jürgen Klopp was the current manager as of September 2020, after taking over on October 8, 2015.

3. Kenny Dalglish first served as the team's manager from May 30, 1985, to February 21, 1991. He then took over again on January 8, 2011, from Roy Hodgson until May 16, 2012. In total, Dalglish was in charge for 381 games with a record of 222 wins, 95 draws, and 64 defeats for a winning percentage of 58.27. He also helped the squad win a total of 10 combined trophies during his stints.

4. In April 1992, manager Graeme Souness underwent heart surgery. Ronnie Moran then took over as caretaker/manager of the side until the 1992 FA Cup Final. Moran led the team to four wins, a draw, and five defeats in his 10 games in charge. Also, manager Gerard Houllier took a leave of absence from the club between October 2001 and February 2002 because of illness. Phil Thompson then took over as The Reds' temporary manager and posted a record of 16 wins, 12 draws, and five losses in 33 contests.

5. After playing with Liverpool between 1946 and 1954, Bob Paisley served as assistant manager between 1959 and 1974 before taking over from Bill Shankly as manager until 1983. Paisley led the team to three European Cups/Champions Leagues victories and is one of two men in history, along with Zinedine Zidane, to do so with the same club as of 2020. He helped the side capture 20 pieces of silverware in nine years, which also included three League Cups, six league championships, a UEFA Cup, and UEFA Super Cup. He also earned six runners-up medals in various competitions.

6. When it comes to their nationalities, 11 Liverpool managers have hailed from England (Tom Watson, David Ashworth, George Patterson, George Kay, Don Welsh, Phil Taylor, Bob Paisley, Joe Fagan, Ronnie Moran, Roy Evans, and Roy Hodgson). Four came from Scotland (Matt McQueen, Bill Shankly, Kenny Dalglish, and Graeme Souness). William Edward Barclay and John McKenna were both from the Republic of Ireland, Brendan Rodgers

is Northern Irish, Rafael Benitez is Spanish, Gerard Houllier is French, and Jürgen Klopp is German.

7. Bill Shankly (December 1, 1959, to July 12, 1974) currently holds the Liverpool record for most games as manager, with 783 under his belt. He also has the most wins with 407 and draws at 198. Tom Watson (August 17, 1896, to May 6, 1915) lost the most contests at 272. The former manager with the best winning percentage was Kenny Dalglish at 58.27. Bob Paisley won the most trophies, with 20, for a rate of 2.2 per season and was named the Manager of the Year in the English top flight a record six times.

8. The shortest reign in club history for a full-time manager was 31 games. This record currently belongs to Roy Hodgson who took over on July 1, 2010, and lasted until January 8, 2011. During this time, he posted a record of 13 wins, nine draws, and nine defeats, with a winning percentage of 41.94. The lowest winning percentage belongs to Don Welsh, who was in the hot seat from March 23, 1951, to May 4, 1956. He had a mark of 81 wins, 58 draws, and 93 losses in 232 outings for a winning percentage of 34.91.

9. Managers Rafael Benitez and Jose Mourinho both made their debuts in the English Premier League in 2004-05, with Benitez at Liverpool and Mourinho at Chelsea. Both liked to play mind games and often got on each other's case. Mourinho typically came out on top when the teams

faced off in the league, but Benitez usually had the upper hand when meeting in other competitions. Benitez once called Chelsea boring, with Mourinho firing back by asking what had Benitez won. Both managed Inter Milan during their careers, and Benitez also took over at Chelsea when Mourinho left, with Mourinho then returning to Chelsea when Benitez was let go.

10. Rafael Benitez also had a running feud with Manchester United manager Sir Alex Ferguson. This was natural, of course, since the teams are archrivals, and it led to Ferguson labeling Liverpool unimaginative and claiming Benitez's defensive tactics were ruining the sport. Ferguson later wrote in his autobiography that Benitez turned their rivalry into a personal one rather than sports related. Benitez used "facts" to criticize Ferguson during an infamous 2009 rant, and when asked to comment on his rival's book, said he didn't want to give Ferguson any undeserved publicity.

CHAPTER 4:

GOALTENDING GREATS

QUIZ TIME!

1. How many goals did Brad Jones concede in his 15 appearances for Liverpool in 2012-13?

    a. 16

    b. 21

    c. 10

    d. 32

2. Which goalkeeper is credited with helping Liverpool win their first-ever league title?

    a. Harry Storer

    b. Matt McQueen

    c. Bill Perkins

    d. Peter Platt

3. As of 2020, 165 goalkeepers have made at least one appearance for The Reds.

    a. True

    b. False

4. Which keeper has made the most appearances in all competitions for the club?

    a. Bruce Grobbelaar

    b. Elisha Scott

    c. Pepe Reina

    d. Ray Clemence

5. How many saves did Jerzy Dudek make in the 2003-04 Premier League?

    a. 90

    b. 88

    c. 84

    d. 93

6. Which keeper was criticized for his play in the 2018 Champions League Final?

    a. Alex Manninger

    b. Danny Ward

    c. Simon Mignolet

    d. Loris Karius

7. Which keeper played 2,610 minutes in Liverpool's first season in the Premier League?

    a. Bruce Grobbelaar

    b. Sander Westerveld

    c. David James

    d. Mike Hooper

8. Matt McQueen won a Second Division championship medal as an outfield player and also won one as a goalkeeper.

a. True

b. False

9. Which keeper allowed 404 goals in 390 matches in all competitions?

   a. Tommy Lawrence

   b. Sam Hardy

   c. Kenneth Campbell

   d. Tommy Younger

10. How many goals did Brad Friedel allow in his 25 Premier League matches with Liverpool?

    a. 30

    b. 27

    c. 32

    d. 40

11. The club used five different keepers in at least one match in 2019-20 competitions.

    a. True

    b. False

12. Who won three of their six appearances across all competitions in 2015-16?

    a. Brad Jones

    b. Alex Manninger

    c. Loris Karius

    d. Ádám Bogdán

13. How many clean sheets did David James tally with the club in domestic league matches?

a. 71

b. 75

c. 66

d. 73

14. Arthur Riley holds the record for the most conceded goals in Liverpool's history.

    a. True

    b. False

15. How many clean sheets did Pepe Reina record with Liverpool?

    a. 170

    b. 154

    c. 163

    d. 161

16. In 338 appearances, how many goals did Arthur Riley allow?

    a. 590

    b. 645

    c. 608

    d. 534

17. Which keeper made 72 saves in the 2019-20 Premier League?

    a. Loris Karius

    b. Alisson

    c. Caoimhin Kelleher

    d. Adrián

18. Sander Westerveld won how many domestic league matches in 2000-01?

    a. 14
    b. 9
    c. 17
    d. 20

19. Who was Liverpool's lone keeper in the 2013-14 Premier League?

    a. Pepe Reina
    b. Danny Ward
    c. Brad Jones
    d. Simon Mignolet

20. Brazilian keeper Alisson played 4,590 minutes across all competitions in 2018-19.

    a. True
    b. False

QUIZ ANSWERS

1. B – 21

2. C – Bill Perkins

3. B – False

4. D – Ray Clemence

5. B – 88

6. D – Loris Karius

7. C – David James

8. A – True

9. A – Tommy Lawrence

10. C – 32

11. B – False

12. D – Ádám Bogdán

13. A – 71

14. B – False

15. C – 163

16. C – 608

17. B – Alisson

18. D – 20

19. D – Simon Mignolet

20. A – True

DID YOU KNOW?

1. Former Liverpool goalkeeper and English international David James currently holds the all-time Premier League record for appearances by a keeper at 572, with 169 of them being clean sheets. He played 214 league matches with The Reds and 277 in total between 1992 and 1999. James helped the club win the League Cup in 1994-95 before being sold to Aston Villa in June of 1999. He also made 53 appearances for England and was the nation's first black goalkeeper to play in a senior international match.

2. Belgian international Simon Mignolet's career with Liverpool was a bit of a roller coaster ride as fans were originally excited about his potential, but then became frustrated with his mistakes. However, the club loyally stuck with Mignolet as their number-one keeper for a lengthy period of time and gave him a short run as team captain. Mignolet appeared in 204 contests between 2013 and 2019, saved a club-record eight career penalties, and helped the squad win the 2018-19 European Champions League.

3. Former English international Ray Clemence holds The Reds' record for appearances by a keeper with a total of 665 under his belt between 1967 and 1981. He helped the side capture five First Division titles, an FA Cup, a League

Cup, three European Cups, a UEFA Cup, and a European Super Cup. Clemence played 61 times for England and appeared in over 1,000 competitive games during his pro career from 1965 to 1988.

4. Bruce Grobbelaar, who was born in South Africa and grew up in Zimbabwe, holds the Liverpool club record for most games played by a non-British-born player and goalkeeper. He appeared in 626 matches between 1981 and 1994, which is the second-most for a Reds keeper behind Ray Clemence. He helped the outfit win six league championships, three FA Cups, three League Cups, and the 1983-84 European Cup.

5. Other Liverpool keepers who were born in South Africa were Arthur Riley, Dirk Kemp, and Doug Rudham. Riley played 338 times between 1925 and 1939, while Kemp appeared 30 times between 1937 and 1939, and Rudham played 66 matches between 1954 and 1959. The Reds have also had keepers hail from England, Australia, Argentina, Brazil, Germany, America, Spain, Ireland, Belgium, Poland, Wales, Holland, and Scotland.

6. The oldest player to appear in a competitive game for the club was goalkeeper Ned Doig. When he played against Newcastle United on April 11, 1908, he was 41 years and 165 days old. He was also the oldest player to debut for the club when he took his place in goal against Burton United on September 1, 1904, at the age of 37 years and 307 days. The Scottish international helped The Reds win the

Division Two title in 1904-05 and played just over 50 league games for the team.

7. When it comes to Liverpool's longest-serving player, goalkeeper Elisha Scott currently holds the record. The former international from Northern Ireland was with the club for a total of 21 years and 52 days between 1912 and 1934. Scott's career was interrupted by World War I, however, and he helped the team win the First Division crown in 1921-22 and 1922-23. He played over 460 games with the team and later entered the world of football management.

8. Spanish international "Pepe" Reina was another long-serving keeper with The Reds, as he appeared in just under 400 contests between 2005 and 2014. Reina is the son of former Atlético Madrid and Barcelona goalie Miguel Reina and helped the team win the 2005 UEFA Super Cup in his debut. He went on to win the 2006 FA Cup by saving three of four West Ham United penalties in the shootout. He was the club's first-choice keeper for eight seasons before being loaned to Napoli of Italy in 2013-14. He then moved permanently to Bayern Munich in 2014.

9. Sam Hardy, who made 240 appearances for Liverpool between 1905 and 1912, was considered one of the best goalkeepers of his era. He was signed for £500 from Chesterfield and quickly established himself as the team's number-one keeper. He helped the club win the First Division title in 1905-06 and played 21 times with the

English national team. Hardy came from a footballing family as he was related to former Nottingham Forest manager Stan Hardy, while his son Jack, grandson Sam, cousins Harry and Ernest, and nephew Edgar all became footballers.

10. Goalkeeper Jerzy Dudek joined Liverpool in August 2001 and soon became the number-one keeper by helping the side finish second in the Premier League and being nominated for the UEFA Goalkeeper of the Year award. Dudek became just the third Polish player to win the Champions League when The Reds took the crown in 2005 and was again nominated as UEFA's Goalkeeper of the Year. A novelty song called "Du the Dudek" was released in the UK and became a Top 40 hit. He also won the 2003 League Cup and 2005 FA Cup with Liverpool, and played 186 games before heading to Real Madrid in 2007.

CHAPTER 5:

DARING DEFENDERS

QUIZ TIME!

1. Which defender made the most career appearances for Liverpool?

    a. Tommy Smith
    b. Phil Neal
    c. Jamie Carragher
    d. Emlyn Hughes

2. How many yellow cards did Álvaro Arbeloa receive in all competitions in 2008-09?

    a. 13
    b. 7
    c. 12
    d. 9

3. Virgil van Dijk played 3,420 minutes in 2019-20 Premier League matches.

    a. True
    b. False

4. How many league goals did Sami Hyypiä score in his Liverpool career?

   a. 28
   b. 6
   c. 22
   d. 9

5. Which defender had four assists in the 2015-16 Premier League?

   a. Nathaniel Clyne
   b. Alberto Moreno
   c. Dejan Lovren
   d. Mamadou Sakho

6. Jamie Carragher appeared in a total of how many matches for the club?

   a. 725
   b. 688
   c. 740
   d. 737

7. Which defender scored a hat trick against Birmingham City on April 26, 1986?

   a. Alan Kennedy
   b. Gary Ablett
   c. Steve Nicol
   d. Gary Gillespie

8. Chris Lawler holds the club record for most goals by a defender in all competitions.

a. True

b. False

9. How many goals did Chris Lawler score for the club?

a. 38

b. 61

c. 53

d. 42

10. Which defender started their career with Liverpool as a forward?

a. Willie Steel

b. Robert Done

c. Bobby Robinson

d. James Jackson

11. In 1992-93, Liverpool had 10 defenders appear in at least one match.

a. True

b. False

12. Which defender recorded four assists in 2005-06 domestic league games?

a. Steve Finnan

b. Jan Kromkamp

c. John Arne Riise

d. Stephen Warnock

13. In 2017-18, which player completed a total of 1,546 passes?

a. Joe Gomez

b. Andrew Robertson

c. Joël Matip

d. Dejan Lovren

14. Stéphane Henchoz scored two goals with only five shots on target in 1999-2000 domestic league matches.

    a. True

    b. False

15. How many goals did Ron Yeats score in his Liverpool career?

    a. 16

    b. 10

    c. 12

    d. 17

16. Which defender led the club in assists in all competitions in 1996-97?

    a. Mark Wright

    b. Stig Inge Bjørnebye

    c. Neil Ruddock

    d. Bjørn Tore Kvarme

17. Who was given six yellow cards across all competitions in 1998-99?

    a. Bjørn Tore Kvarme

    b. Steve Harkness

    c. Rigobert Song

    d. Phil Babb

18. How many goals did Mark Wright score in his Reds career?

a. 7

b. 8

c. 9

d. 10

19. Which Liverpool defender infamously used his hand (without being penalized) to deflect a shot by Thierry Henry in the 2001 FA Cup Final?

a. Christian Ziege

b. Frode Kippe

c. Stéphane Henchoz

d. Markus Babbel

20. A total of 14 defenders appeared in at least one match for the club in 2015-16.

a. True

b. False

QUIZ ANSWERS

1. C – Jamie Carragher

2. C – 12

3. A – True

4. C – 22

5. B – Alberto Moreno

6. D – 737

7. D – Gary Gillespie

8. A – True

9. B – 61

10. C – Bobby Robinson

11. B – False

12. A – Steve Finnan

13. D – Dejan Lovren

14. B – False

15. A – 16

16. B – Stig Inge Bjørnebye

17. D – Phil Babb

18. C – 9

19. C – Stéphane Henchoz

20. A – True

DID YOU KNOW?

1. Defender Julian Dicks played fewer than 30 games with Liverpool in 1993-94 but became a fan favorite as he was signed to give the squad some toughness. He was a hard tackler who was known as "The Terminator" because of his tough playing style. However, he was also a skilled footballer who specialized at free kicks and penalties, achieving 69 career goals and a couple of caps with the England B Team. Dicks asked to be transferred in 1994 after constant criticism from manager Roy Evans and headed back to West Ham United, where Liverpool originally signed him from.

2. Another rough and tumble defender was Neil "Razor" Ruddock, as he often cut opposing players down on the pitch. The punishing player appeared in 152 Liverpool games from 1993 to 1998 after arriving from Tottenham Hotspur and leaving for West Ham United. He often put aside his skills to play a robust, physical style of game and had some famous disagreements on the pitch during his career with opponents such as Eric Cantona, Patrick Vieira, Peter Beardsley, and Andy Cole. When opposing players ventured down Ruddock's part of the pitch, it was done at their own risk.

3. The club record for most appearances by a defender, and second overall by any player, is 737 by Jamie Carragher,

49

who played his entire pro career with Liverpool between 1996 and 2013. Carragher played in over 500 league games and wasn't worried about scoring as he notched just five goals in his Reds career. Carragher also played 38 times for England, as well as a club-high 150 times for Liverpool in European competitions. He helped the team win a Champions League medal, a UEFA Cup, three League Cups, and a pair of Super Cups and FA Cups.

4. Even though defender Paul Konchesky was bought from Fulham by his former manager Roy Hodgson for just under £4 million in 2010, he was generally considered to be a bit of a disappointment with Liverpool. The former English international was brought in to solidify the team's defense but played just a total of 18 mainly error-prone games with them and soon attracted the ire of Reds supporters. He was sent on loan with Nottingham Forest in January 2011 and then signed with Leicester City six months later.

5. Robert "Bobby" Robinson notched 65 goals in 271 games for Liverpool from 1904 to 1912, and although he may be considered a defender, there's more to the story. Robinson was signed by manager Tom Watson as a forward, and he scored a team-high 23 goals in 32 outings in 1904-05 to win the Second Division and earn promotion back to the top flight after being relegated a year earlier. Robinson also helped the side win the First Division in 1905-06 and was then asked to play as a defender for the rest of his days with the club. His goal output may have dried up, but he

was able to extend his Reds career by a few seasons by playing in the back.

6. The highest-scoring pure defender in club history so far as been Chris Lawler, with 61 goals in 549 outings between 1963 and 1975. The former English international right-back thought like a striker and helped Liverpool win the FA Cup for the first time in 1965. He played 316 straight games between October 2, 1965, and April 24, 1971, and also helped the team win the First Division in 1965-66 and 1972-73, with another FA Cup medal in 1974 and a UEFA Cup in 1973.

7. Mark Lawrenson was an Irish international defender who played 356 times for The Reds and helped the club capture five First Division titles, three League Cups, an FA Cup, a Football League Super Cup, and the European Cup. Lawrenson was bought for £900,000 in 1981 from Brighton & Hove Albion and formed a solid central defensive pairing with Alan Hansen and also played left-back. After hanging up his boots, Lawrenson became involved in football management and then television broadcasting.

8. Central defender Alan Hansen cost Liverpool just £100,000 in 1977 and would go on to play 620 games with the club from 1977 to 1990, with 14 goals to his credit. He helped the squad capture eight top-flight league titles, three European Cups, three League Cups, two FA Cups, and a European Super Cup. The Scottish international was nicknamed "Jocky" and was famous for not wilting under

pressure. He was acquired from Partick Thistle in his homeland and was also an accomplished athlete at volleyball, golf, and squash.

9. Former captain Sami Hyypiä was signed in 1999 for £2.6 million and became one of the club's biggest bargains ever. Typically playing alongside Stéphane Henchoz or Jamie Carragher, Hyypiä was as tough as they come but received just one red card in his pro career. The Finnish international played with The Reds from 1999 to 2009 and contributed 35 goals in 464 games. He also helped the team lift two FA Cups, two League Cups, a UEFA Cup, the European Champions League Cup, and two European Super Cups.

10. Although he played just one international match for England, Tommy Smith enjoyed a 16-year career with Liverpool between 1963 and 1978. He chipped in to win four league titles, two FA Cups, two UEFA Cups, the European Super Cup, and the European Cup. He tallied 48 goals in 638 contests. The former Reds skipper was known as "The Anfield Iron" and would later play in America before retiring in 1979.

CHAPTER 6:

MAESTROS OF THE MIDFIELD

QUIZ TIME!

1. Which midfielder led the club with 14 assists in 2014-15 Premier League matches?

    a. Brad Smith
    b. Steven Gerrard
    c. Lucas Leiva
    d. Joe Allen

2. How many goals did John Barnes score in all competitions in 1989-90?

    a. 18
    b. 30
    c. 22
    d. 28

3. Jordan Henderson made his Liverpool debut in a Europa League match.

    a. True
    b. False

4. Which midfielder has made the most appearances in the club's history?

   a. Peter Thompson
   b. Ronnie Whelan
   c. Ian Callaghan
   d. Steven Gerrard

5. Who played 2,802 minutes across all competitions in 1993-94?

   a. Jan Mølby
   b. Nigel Clough
   c. Jamie Redknapp
   d. Steve McManaman

6. How many yellow cards did Xabi Alonso receive in 2006-07 Premier League matches?

   a. 7
   b. 10
   c. 8
   d. 9

7. How many career appearances did Ian Callaghan make with Liverpool?

   a. 857
   b. 849
   c. 853
   d. 862

8. Georginio Wijnaldum led the club in assists across all competitions in 2016-17.

a. True

b. False

9. Who was the only midfielder to score a penalty kick for Liverpool in 2011-12?

    a. Jay Spearing

    b. Jordan Henderson

    c. Charlie Adam

    d. Steven Gerrard

10. How many total matches did Terry McDermott play for The Reds?

    a. 229

    b. 296

    c. 361

    d. 329

11. Steven Gerrard holds the club record for most goals by a midfielder as of 2020.

    a. True

    b. False

12. How many goals did Ian Callaghan tally with the club?

    a. 67

    b. 68

    c. 107

    d. 110

13. Which midfielder did NOT receive a red card in any competition in 2002-03?

a. Steven Gerrard

b. Dietmar Hamann

c. Salif Diao

d. Bruno Cheyrou

14. Raheem Sterling scored 20 goals in 2013-14.

   a. True

   b. False

15. Of Fabinho's 41 total matches played in 2018-19, how many of them were starts?

   a. 37

   b. 24

   c. 30

   d. 28

16. How many career goals did Steven Gerrard score with the club?

   a. 172

   b. 153

   c. 186

   d. 190

17. Who led the squad with 10 assists in all competitions in 2001-02?

   a. Danny Murphy

   b. Dietmar Hamann

   c. Patrik Berger

   d. Gary McAllister

18. How many goals did Charlie Adam score in 37 games with the team from 2011 to 2012?

   a. 7
   b. 12
   c. 8
   d. 2

19. Which midfielder scored 11 goals in the 1992-93 domestic league?

   a. Jamie Redknapp
   b. Mark Walters
   c. Don Hutchison
   d. Steve McManaman

20. In 2019-20, a total of 14 midfielders appeared in at least one match for Liverpool.

   a. True
   b. False

QUIZ ANSWERS

1. B – Steven Gerrard

2. D – 28

3. B – False

4. C – Ian Callaghan

5. C – Jamie Redknapp

6. D – 9

7. A – 857

8. A – True

9. C – Charlie Adam

10. D – 329

11. B – False

12. B – 68

13. D – Bruno Cheyrou

14. B – False

15. C – 30

16. C – 186

17. A – Danny Murphy

18. D – 2

19. B – Mark Walters

20. A – True

DID YOU KNOW?

1. Liverpool legend Ian Callaghan made the most appearances for the club at 857 between 1960 and 1978 and contributed 68 goals. He managed to earn several major honors and was also a member of England's 1966 World Cup winning squad. He debuted as a right-winger and then moved to central midfield early in the 1970s. He helped the club win a Second Division title, five First Division crowns, two FA Cups, two European Cups, two UEFA Cups, and a UEFA Super Cup. Callaghan also won a Football Writers' Footballer of the Year award and was awarded the MBE for services to football.

2. Steven Gerrard was a tenacious midfielder and former club captain who spent his entire Premier League career with the team between 1998 and 2015. The inspirational leader had a knack for scoring big goals and always took matters into his own hands when his side was in trouble. He scored at least one goal in a League Cup, FA Cup, UEFA Cup, and Champions League Final and notched 186 goals in 710 appearances with 21 goals in 114 games with England. He joined the Liverpool academy at nine years old, played in America after leaving the club, and is currently a football manager.

3. Spanish international midfielder Xabi Alonso was a hit at Anfield by helping the club win an FA Cup, UEFA Super Cup, and European Champions League title before moving

on to Real Madrid where he won another boatload of trophies. Alonso appeared with The Reds in 210 games between 2005 and 2009, with 19 goals and 19 assists to his name. He was strong in defense, comfortable in possession with great vision and passing skills, and a tremendous tackler.

4. Liverpool acquired Stewart Downing in July 2011 for a reported £20 million from Aston Villa, and although he was an English international, his days at Anfield were numbered from the start. He struggled with the squad and manager Brendan Rodgers's system and was sometimes inserted into the lineup at left-back. Downing played just 91 games with the club over two seasons before being sold to West Ham United for a reported £5 million. Downing scored seven times for The Reds with a League Cup win in 2012, and at the end of 2019-20, had 63 goals in 703 pro career games.

5. In January 2013, Liverpool paid £8.5 million to Inter Milan for the services of Brazilian international Philippe Coutinho, and it turned into one of the steals of the century. He excelled at Anfield and became known as "The Magician." He was named to the PFA Team of the Year in 2015 and won several other individual club honors during his stint. Coutinho banged in 54 goals in 201 appearances and was credited with 43 assists. After asking for a transfer, he became the second-most expensive player in the world when Liverpool sold him to Barcelona for a reported £142 million.

6. John Barnes moved to England from his homeland of Jamaica as a youngster and became a star at Anfield as well as a valuable member of England's national team. He was an excellent dribbler and was the first high-profile black player with the club after being acquired from Watford for £900,000 in June 1987. Barnes combined strength, speed, and skill and chipped in with 108 goals and 101 assists in 408 contests with the club. He was the Professional Writers' Player of the Year twice and helped the side win two league titles, an FA Cup, and a League Cup.

7. Scottish international Graeme Souness may have scored 55 goals in 359 outings with Liverpool and was a former captain, but he's best known for his no-nonsense approach to the game. Souness was as tough as they come but also possessed some delicate footballing skills. He helped the team win 15 pieces of silverware between 1978 and 1984 after being bought from Middlesbrough for £352,000, which was then a record fee between two English sides. This includes three European Cups and five league titles. The "Emperor of Anfield" left Liverpool for Italy but returned later to manage at Anfield.

8. On Christmas Eve, 1897, The Reds paid the considerable amount of £150 to Blackpool for the services of Irish international Jack Cox after he tallied 12 goals in 17 games with the Second Division side. He soon became a regular and helped the team capture league championships in 1900-01 and 1905-06 and contributed 81 goals in 360

appearances. He was a tricky and speedy player who rejoined Blackpool in 1909 on a free transfer to become the team's player/manager and then retired in 1911.

9. Hometown boy Jimmy Case played with Liverpool between 1975 and 1981 and posted 46 goals in 269 outings. In addition, he helped the squad lift four league championships, three European Cups, a UEFA Cup, a European Super Cup, and a League Cup. Case took no prisoners as a tough-tackling midfielder and owned a tremendous shot. He was noticed by Reds scouts when playing non-league football with South Liverpool and took two weeks off of work to attend a trial with the club. Case turned The Reds down when they offered to sign him as he wanted to finish his electrician's apprenticeship. He then signed as a full-time pro at the age of 20.

10. Patrik Berger was a Czech Republic international who was known for his long-range shooting, silky smooth dribbling, and pinpoint passing ability. He registered 35 goals and 24 assists with the club in 196 outings between 1996 and 2003 and won an FA Cup and UEFA Cup. Berger attracted Liverpool at the 1996 European Championships in England when his nation lost the Final to Germany. He scored twice in his debut as a starter and was the league's Player of the Month to kick off his Reds career. Berger then headed to Portsmouth in 2003.

CHAPTER 7:

SENSATIONAL STRIKERS/FORWARDS

QUIZ TIME!

1. Who led the club with 18 goals in the 1997-98 Premier League?

    a. Paul Ince

    b. Karl-Heinz Riedle

    c. Robbie Fowler

    d. Michael Owen

2. How many goals did Luis Suárez score in the 2013-14 domestic league?

    a. 26

    b. 11

    c. 23

    d. 31

3. Jari Litmanen notched nine goals in 43 total appearances for the club.

    a. True

    b. False

4. How many domestic league goals did Erik Meijer score in his brief time with the team?

   a. 6

   b. 1

   c. 0

   d. 8

5. Which player scored twice in the 1974 FA Cup Final, a feat which had not been done since 1966?

   a. Alan Waddle

   b. Kevin Keegan

   c. John Toshack

   d. Jack Whitman

6. Who recorded a total of 16 assists in 2017-18?

   a. Philippe Coutinho

   b. Sadio Mané

   c. Roberto Firmino

   d. Mohamed Salah

7. Which player holds the record for most hat tricks in team history?

   a. Michael Owen

   b. Roger Hunt

   c. Ian Rush

   d. Gordon Hodgson

8. Robbie Fowler famously scored one of the fastest hat tricks in the Premier League in 4 minutes 33 seconds.

   a. True

   b. False

9. How many appearances did it take Kenny Dalglish to score his 172 goals with the club?

    a. 515
    b. 498
    c. 511
    d. 476

10. Who scored four penalty kicks in 1998-99 domestic league games?

    a. Titi Camara
    b. Karl-Heinz Riedle
    c. Robbie Fowler
    d. Sean Dundee

11. Billy Liddell played for Liverpool for 25 seasons.

    a. True
    b. False

12. Which player tallied 4,511 minutes of play in all competitions in 2014-15?

    a. Philippe Coutinho
    b. Raheem Sterling
    c. Adam Lallana
    d. Lazar Marković

13. Roger Hunt holds the club record of most career league goals with how many?

    a. 232
    b. 256
    c. 235
    d. 244

14. John Aldridge scored 63 goals in domestic league matches for Liverpool in 104 appearances.

    a. True

    b. False

15. In only 44 league appearances with Liverpool, how many goals did Andy Carroll score?

    a. 10

    b. 2

    c. 6

    d. 4

16. How many goals did Mohamed Salah score across all competitions in his first year with The Reds?

    a. 43

    b. 32

    c. 26

    d. 19

17. During his Liverpool career, how many goals did Ian Rush score in all competitions?

    a. 339

    b. 346

    c. 351

    d. 340

18. How many forwards appeared in at least one match in 2000-01?

    a. 4

    b. 6

c. 8

d. 9

19. Who recorded 10 yellow cards in the 2012-13 Premier League?

    a. Stewart Downing

    b. Daniel Sturridge

    c. Luis Suárez

    d. Raheem Sterling

20. Fernando Torres notched over 100 career goals in all competitions for Liverpool.

    a. True

    b. False

QUIZ ANSWERS

1. D – Michael Owen

2. D – 31

3. A – True

4. C – 0

5. B – Kevin Keegan

6. C – Roberto Firmino

7. D – Gordon Hodgson

8. A – True

9. A – 515

10. C – Robbie Fowler

11. B – False

12. B – Raheem Sterling

13. D – 244

14. B – False

15. C – 6

16. A – 43

17. B – 346

18. C – 8

19. C – Luis Suárez

20. B – False

DID YOU KNOW?

1. Striker Rickie Lambert won two Golden Boots and scored 241 goals during his pro career and notched three goals in 11 games for England, including scoring on his first touch. He also won numerous personal awards, but just three goals came in 36 appearances for The Reds. Lambert, who was born in Liverpool, was in the club's youth system as a 10-year-old but was let go five years later. Liverpool then bought him from Southampton in June 2014 to fulfill his lifelong dream of playing at Anfield. He managed to score a goal in all four English pro divisions as well as the European Champions League and for the national team.

2. Peter Crouch was another English international striker who played with Liverpool after being bought from Southampton. He tallied 42 goals and 17 assists with the team in 134 games between 2005 and 2008 and added 22 goals in 42 appearances for England. At 6 feet 7 inches tall, Crouch was one of the tallest players around and was of course quite good in the air. However, his skillful ball control and sublime goals on the ground surprised many fans as did his infamous robot-dance goal celebration.

3. Let's not forget Emile Heskey either, as he was credited with 60 goals and 26 assists with Liverpool between March 2000 and 2004. He was bought for a reported £11 million from Leicester City, his hometown, which was a club-record transfer fee at the time. The powerfully built 6-foot-

2-inch striker also deposited the ball into the net seven times in 62 contests with England. Heskey helped the side win two League Cups, an FA Cup, a UEFA Cup, and a UEFA Super Cup. He was sold to Birmingham City in 2004 and would later play in Australia.

4. Italian international Mario Balotelli was always quite interesting and a bit of a cult figure and was once labeled "unmanageable" by manager Jose Mourinho while playing at Inter Milan. He always had the potential to be a world-class striker, and Liverpool realized that when they paid a reported £16 million to Milan for him in August 2014. Balotelli struggled to earn starts under manager Brendan Rodgers, though, and played just 28 games with the club and landed four goals. He was then returned to Milan on loan. As of September 2020, Balotelli had 14 goals in 36 outings for Italy and 151 markers in his pro club career.

5. When Stan Collymore was bought from Nottingham Forest in 1995 for £8.5 million, it set a new transfer record for an English player. Collymore's pro career lasted from 1991 to 2001 when he retired at the age of 30. He netted over 100 goals in 259 contests before becoming a television personality and dabbling in acting, even appearing in the movie *Basic Instinct 2* with actress Sharon Stone. He tallied 35 of his goals in 81 outings with Liverpool, with 16 assists. Collymore played three times for England and was sold in May 1997 to Aston Villa for a Villa record of £7 million.

6. There was tremendous hype and excitement at Anfield when Spanish international Fernando Morientes arrived in January 2005 from Real Madrid. The club paid £6.3 million for his services, which made him one their biggest signings in recent years. However, he managed just eight goals in 41 league games and a dozen in 61 contests in all competitions. Morientes then promptly headed back to Spain in May 2006 and joined Valencia. He finished his career with 27 goals in 47 games with Spain and 208 career club goals.

7. Robbie Fowler was one of the Premier League's greatest strikers and became a fan favorite due to his somewhat cheeky personality. He scored 254 career club goals in 590 games in England, Australia, and Thailand, with 183 of them coming in 369 contests with Liverpool. Nicknamed "God" with the club, Fowler enjoyed two stints at Anfield from 1993 to 2001 and 2006 to 2007. He was part of the historic treble winning side in 2000-01 which won the League Cup, FA Cup, and UEFA Cup. And also won the League Cup in 1994-95 and the 2001 UEFA Super Cup.

8. Arguably, Michael Owen of Liverpool was the best player on the planet in 2000-01 when he was honored as the European Footballer of the Year and English PFA Young Player of the Year. Owen was fifth in Premier League scoring that campaign, with 16 goals, but tallied 24 in 46 outings to lead the squad. Owen led the team to the FA Cup, League Cup, and the UEFA Cup that season and finished his Liverpool career with 158 goals and 41 assists

in 297 appearances from 1997 to 2004. Owen, who tallied 40 goals in 89 games for England, also won another League Cup and a European Super Cup with the team.

9. The word prolific has often been used to describe former Republic of Ireland international Robbie Keane. He enjoyed a fantastic career which saw him score consistently at every club. He holds his nation's record for international goals, with 68, and appearances at 146. Keane notched another 325 goals in 737 career club contests but managed just seven markers and five assists in 28 games with Liverpool in 2008-09. He was bought from Tottenham in July 2008 for a reported £19 million and sold back to the club for £12 million just six months later.

10. Liverpool-born Jack Balmer's uncles Bob and Walter played with Everton in the early 1900s, but Jack played with Liverpool between 1935 and 1952 and scored 111 goals in 312 appearances. The former captain helped the team win the league title in 1946-47 following World War II when he scored 24 goals to end the team's 24-year league-title drought. Balmer scored three straight hat tricks during the campaign to set a club record, including one in six minutes. He ended up scoring 10 consecutive goals and added another five in his next four outings for 15 goals in seven games. Balmer also scored in his one and only game for England.

CHAPTER 8:

NOTABLE TRANSFERS/SIGNINGS

QUIZ TIME!

1. What was the reported price paid to acquire goalkeeper Alisson Becker from Roma in 2018?

    a. £65 million

    b. £58.5 million

    c. £46.8 million

    d. £70 million

2. In 2015-16, the club sold which player for a reported fee of £49 million?

    a. Steven Gerrard

    b. Raheem Sterling

    c. Fabio Borini

    d. Rickie Lambert

3. In 2013, Liverpool signed Philippe Coutinho for a reported £8.5 million.

    a. True

    b. False

4. Which player did Liverpool sell to Crystal Palace in 2016 for a reported £32 million?

    a. Christian Benteke

    b. Jerome Sinclair

    c. Jordon Ibe

    d. Martin Škrtel

5. Who was the only player the club sold in 1986-87?

    a. Alan Irvine

    b. Steve Staunton

    c. Sammy Lee

    d. Nigel Spackman

6. How much did Liverpool reportedly sell Luis Suárez to F.C. Barcelona for in 2014?

    a. £54.6 million

    b. £47 million

    c. £32.9 million

    d. £65 million

7. Who did the club sell to AFC Bournemouth in 2018-19?

    a. Danny Ward

    b. Jon Flanagan

    c. Dominic Solanke

    d. Ragnar Klavan

8. Liverpool spent a total of £118 million in the 2019 transfer market.

    a. True

    b. False

9. Which player did the club spend a reported £3.5 million on in 2015-16?

   a. Joe Gomez

   b. Danny Ings

   c. Marko Grujić

   d. James Milner

10. Liverpool paid a reported fee of how much to acquire Djibril Cissé in 2004?

    a. £10.7 million

    b. £6.5 million

    c. £8 million

    d. £14.5 million

11. The Reds spent £500,000 to acquire Aly Cissokho in 2013-14.

    a. True

    b. False

12. Liverpool sold which player to Fiorentina in 2012?

    a. Charlie Adam

    b. Dirk Kuyt

    c. Doni

    d. Alberto Aquilani

13. The club signed which player from Newcastle United in 1987?

    a. John Aldridge

    b. Ray Houghton

    c. Peter Beardsley

    d. John Barnes

14. Liverpool first acquired striker Ian Rush from Chester in 1980.

    a. True
    b. False

15. Who was the club's first signing of the Premier League era?

    a. David James
    b. Stig Inge Bjørnebye
    c. Torben Piechnik
    d. Paul Stewart

16. Which goalkeeper was NOT a free signing by the club?

    a. Adrián
    b. Ádám Bogdán
    c. Loris Karius
    d. Alex Manninger

17. Who has been Liverpool's most expensive acquisition as of September 2020?

    a. Fernando Torres
    b. Naby Keïta
    c. Andy Carroll
    d. Virgil van Dijk

18. Which club did The Reds acquire Mohamed Salah from in 2017?

    a. Roma
    b. ACF Fiorentina
    c. F.C. Basel
    d. Chelsea

19. Which club did Liverpool acquire midfielder Thiago Alcantara from in September 2020?

    a. Real Madrid
    b. Chelsea
    c. Bayern Munich
    d. Paris Saint-Germain

20. Liverpool signed Virgil van Dijk for a reported fee of £100 million.

    a. True
    b. False

QUIZ ANSWERS

1. A – £65 million

2. B – Raheem Sterling

3. A – True

4. A – Christian Benteke

5. C – Sammy Lee

6. D – £65 million

7. C – Dominic Solanke

8. B – False

9. A – Joe Gomez

10. D – £14.5 million

11. B – False

12. D – Alberto Aquilani

13. C – Peter Beardsley

14. A – True

15. A – David James

16. C – Loris Karius

17. D – Virgil van Dijk

18. A – Roma

19. C – Bayern Munich

20. B – False

DID YOU KNOW?

1. Mohamed Salah didn't fit in when playing in England with Chelsea in 2014, but that changed when Liverpool paid a then club-record £43.9 million for him in 2017. The Egyptian international forward set a new Premier League record with 32 goals in 36 outings and won the PFA Players' Player of the Year award for 2017-18. He shared the Golden Boot again the next season and helped the team win the UEFA Champions League, UEFA Super Cup, and FIFA Club World Cup in 2019 and the Premier League in 2019-20. Salah had scored 97 goals in his first 154 games with The Reds, including a hat trick on the opening day of the 2020-21 Premier League.

2. One player who never fit in with The Reds was Italian international midfielder Alberto Aquilani who joined the club for £17 million in 2009 from Roma. He played just 16 games in all competitions in his first season under manager Rafael Benitez with one goal to his name. When Roy Hodgson took over as manager, Aquilani played just twice more for the club and was then sent out on loan to Juventus and AC Milan before eventually being sold to Fiorentina for a fee reportedly below £1 million.

3. Uruguayan international forward Luis Suárez joined Liverpool in January 2011 from Ajax of Amsterdam for a reported £22.8 million, a club record at the time. He made

an instant impact at Anfield and turned the squad into a legitimate league and cup contenders. He won the Golden Boot in 2013-14 with 31 goals in 33 games and was named PFA Player of the Year. Suárez scored 82 goals in 133 outings with The Reds to lead the team three seasons in a row and was named Player of the Year twice while making the Premier League Team of the Year twice.

4. Things turned sour for Luis Suárez at Anfield as he became adamant on leaving even though he had recently signed a new contract. In May 2013, he announced he wanted to leave Liverpool. Arsenal then offered £40 million for him and had the bid rejected. The player threatened to take The Reds to court after claiming manager Brendan Rodgers said he could leave if Liverpool failed to qualify for the European Champions League. This was denied by Rodgers, and Suárez was told to train by himself while club owner John Henry stated he wouldn't be sold. Suárez remained and signed another long-term deal in December 2013 but was eventually sold to Barcelona for £80 million in July 2014.

5. Another Liverpool transfer saga involved Raheem Sterling, who was one of the most exciting young players around in 2015. The 20-year-old, Jamaican-born, English international had enjoyed an excellent start to his pro career at Anfield but wanted a hefty new deal, which the club was unwilling to pay. Sterling turned nasty when manager Brendan Rodgers rejected several transfer bids and criticized the boss publicly. The player soon discovered Manchester City

was willing to pay him £200,000 a week compared to Liverpool's offer of £100,000 and told the club he wouldn't show up for preseason training and team tours in Asia and Australia. He was then sold to Man City for approximately £49 million to set a new high for an English player.

6. Liverpool controversially sold Spanish international striker Fernando Torres to Chelsea in January 2011 for a then British-record £50 million after paying Atletico Madrid a reported £20 million for him in 2007. Torres was a star at Anfield with 81 goals in 142 appearances, including 65 goals in 102 league matches. He asked The Reds for a transfer but may have regretted it after his form went down the drain in London with his new club, with just 20 goals in 110 league contests and 45 markers in 172 games in all competitions.

7. After Fernando Torres was sold to Chelsea in 2011, manager Kenny Dalglish basically found himself without a world-class striker. He then paid a new club-record £35 million to Newcastle United for young English international Andy Carroll, with the fee also being a record for a British player. Carroll produced just six league goals in 44 matches with The Reds, though, after scoring 31 in 80 games with Newcastle. Carroll was then sent to West Ham on loan when Brendan Rodgers took over as manager, and he was eventually sold to the club for a reported £15 million.

8. Liverpool was still looking for a top striker in 2015 to replace the departed Luis Suárez and Andy Carroll and

acquired Belgian international Christian Benteke from Aston Villa for a reported £32.5 million. Reds supporters watched Benteke struggle much the same as Carroll did, and he managed just 10 goals in 42 appearances, with 9 coming in 29 league games. Benteke was known for power and strength, but his inconsistent play resulted in his departure after just one campaign. Benteke was then sold to Crystal Palace in August 2016 for a reported £32 million.

9. Argentine international defender Javier Mascherano was just 22 years old when he arrived at Anfield from West Ham United in January 2007. He was originally acquired on loan and later bought for £18 million. The newcomer quickly helped The Reds form a solid back-four, which also included Spanish international Xabi Alonso, and Mascherano helped The Reds reach the European Champions League Final several months later. He stayed with the club until 2010 when he joined Barcelona and was one of Liverpool's most dependable players due to his passing and tackling skills and ability to play in the midfield.

10. As of September 15, 2020, Liverpool's five most-expensive transfer acquisitions (including clauses in contract) have been: Virgil van Dijk from Southampton for £75 million in January 2018, Goalkeeper Alisson Becker from Roma for £65 million in July 2018, Naby Keïta from Leipzig for £52.75 million in July 2018, Mohamed Salah for £43.9 million from Roma in June 2017, and Fabinho Tavarez from Monaco for £43.7 million in July 2018. The biggest

fees received have been: Philippe Coutinho to Barcelona for £142 million in January 2018, Luis Suárez to Barcelona for £65 million in July 2014, Fernando Torres to Chelsea for £50 million in January 2011, Raheem Sterling to Manchester City for £49 million in July 2015, and Christian Benteke to Crystal Palace for £32 million in August 2016.

CHAPTER 9:

ODDS & ENDS

QUIZ TIME!

1. How many matches did Liverpool win in 2019-20 to claim the Premier League title?

    a. 29
    b. 32
    c. 33
    d. 30

2. Liverpool set a club record for goals in a top-flight season in 2013-14 with how many?

    a. 103
    b. 99
    c. 101
    d. 106

3. In their first campaign in the First Division in 1894, Liverpool finished in last place.

    a. True
    b. False

4. What were Liverpool's original kit colors?

    a. Red and blue
    b. Blue and black
    c. Blue and white
    d. Red and white

5. Which player was nicknamed "The Ghost"?

    a. Michael Owen
    b. John Barnes
    c. Steven Gerrard
    d. Ian Rush

6. In 1953-54, Liverpool set a club record in which category?

    a. Most draws
    b. Most losses
    c. Fewest goals against
    d. Fewest draws

7. How many years did Liverpool go without a trophy before winning the 2019-20 league title?

    a. 30
    b. 25
    c. 32
    d. 27

8. Liverpool did NOT lose a domestic league match in 1893-94.

    a. True
    b. False

9. Which former player was nicknamed "God"?

    a. Roger Hunt
    b. Kevin Keegan
    c. Robbie Fowler
    d. Kenny Dalglish

10. The Merseyside rivalry is between Liverpool and which other club?

    a. Manchester United
    b. Everton
    c. Manchester City
    d. Queens Park Rangers

11. Jack Balmer scored a hat trick in three consecutive domestic league games, the only Liverpool player to do so.

    a. True
    b. False

12. Who is NOT one of the three players to appear in over 200 games and not score an official goal?

    a. Ephraim Longworth
    b. Tom Cooper
    c. Stéphane Henchoz
    d. Rob Jones

13. How many seconds did it take Joe Cole to score a goal against Steaua București in the 2010 Europa League?

    a. 23
    b. 41
    c. 27
    d. 32

14. In 1893, Liverpool was nicknamed "the team with all the Macs" because Scottish players formed most of the roster.

    a. True
    b. False

15. What number did goalkeeper Pepe Reina wear in the 2005 World Club Championship instead of his usual number 25?

    a. 23
    b. 14
    c. 6
    d. 12

16. As of 2020, how many times have Liverpool faced Everton in the FA Cup?

    a. 13
    b. 17
    c. 21
    d. 19

17. Which player scored his only goal for the club in a League Cup Final?

    a. Stephen Warnock
    b. Antonio Núñez
    c. Anthony Le Tallec
    d. Nabil El Zhar

18. How many times did Ian Callaghan receive a yellow card in his Reds career?

    a. 3
    b. 0

c. 1

d. 2

19. What is Liverpool's record for the most defeats in a season?

    a. 25

    b. 19

    c. 23

    d. 21

20. Ian Rush scored at least one goal in each of the matches he played on New Year's Day for Liverpool.

    a. True

    b. False

QUIZ ANSWERS

1. B – 32

2. C – 101

3. A – True

4. C – Blue and white

5. D – Ian Rush

6. B – Most losses

7. A – 30

8. A – True

9. C – Robbie Fowler

10. B – Everton

11. A – True

12. B – Tom Cooper

13. C – 27

14. A – True

15. D – 12

16. D – 19

17. B – Antonio Núñez

18. C – 1

19. C – 23

20. A – True

DID YOU KNOW?

1. Liverpool's most intense rivalry is with Manchester United, with their hostilities known as the North West Derby, and their first historic meeting happened in 1894. Generally, the Liverpool vs. Man United clash is considered the most famous in all of England as it features the country's two most successful football clubs. They have combined for dozens of European, domestic and world-based trophies, with The Reds winning 19 top-flight league titles and The Red Devils taking 10. Liverpool has the edge in Europe though with six European crowns to Man United's three. Man United holds the edge in their derbies, as of September 2020, with 80 wins, 67 defeats, and 57 draws.

2. The Merseyside Derby is the contest between Liverpool and their crosstown rivals Everton F.C., with the clubs' two grounds being only about a mile apart. The first clash took place on October 13, 1894, with Liverpool having the best of it by September 2020, with 93 wins, 75 draws, and 66 defeats. The biggest triumph was Liverpool's 6-0 thrashing of Everton in 1935, while Everton goalkeeper Neville Southall made the most appearances in the derby at 41. The Reds' Ian Rush is currently the derby's top scorer with 25 goals. Although it's also been referred to as "The Friendly Derby," this fixture currently has produced the most red cards in Premier League history.

3. One of the club's finest passers of the ball was Danish international Jan Mølby who also notched 61 goals in 292 games between 1984 and 1995. He was well known for his technique and vision after playing with Dutch legends Johan Cruyff and Marco van Basten with Ajax in 1982-83. He arrived in August 1984 to help fill the void when Graeme Souness left. He scored 21 times in 58 contests in 1985-86 to help The Reds win the League and FA Cups. Mølby scored on 42 of 45 penalty attempts with the team and once tallied a hat trick from the penalty spot in a 1986 League Cup match against Coventry.

4. When Liverpool publicly announced in early July 2008 that they were interested in Republic of Ireland striker Robbie Keane of Tottenham Hotspur, it could have been a mistake. Tottenham then filed an official complaint with the Premier League regarding Liverpool's conduct, claiming the club had unsettled the player. But just a few weeks later, Spurs confirmed the sale of Keane to Liverpool with the player then inking a four-year contract. Once the transfer was signed, sealed, and delivered, Tottenham withdrew their complaint as The Reds apologized for their conduct and also donated a sum of money to the Tottenham Hotspur Foundation.

5. Former Reds striker Mario Balotelli, who was nicknamed "Super Mario," arrived at the club from Italy with a reputation of marching to his own drummer. In a European Champions League match in October 2014 against Real Madrid, Balotelli swapped shirts with

Madrid's Pepe at the half-time break. This incensed manager Brendan Rodgers, who remarked, "It's something that doesn't happen here and shouldn't happen here." This was a tame incident though compared to some of Balotelli's alleged on- and off-field antics over the years.

6. Although it was a long wait to win the Premier League title, Liverpool set several league records along the way to claiming the crown in 2019-20. These included: Most home league wins in a row at 24, with the streak beginning the previous season; the earliest title win by capturing the crown with seven matches remaining; the most points in a 38-game season, with 110; the fastest team to reach 30 wins by achieving it in 34 games; the best Premier League start ever, with 61 points of a possible 63 from their first 21 games and 79 points of a possible 81 in their first 27 contests; most home wins in a season with 18 of 19 to tie several other clubs for this record; most wins in a season with 32, which is also a shared record set by Manchester City.

7. Former English international defender Phil Neal holds the Liverpool record for playing in 417 straight games for the squad between October 23, 1976, and September 24, 1983. Neal, who was nicknamed "Zico," appeared in every minute of every league and cup contest for the equivalent of nine consecutive seasons between 1976-77 and 1983-84. He tallied 59 goals in 650 games with The Reds and helped the side win eight First Division titles, four League Cups, four European Cups, a UEFA Cup, and a UEFA Super Cup.

8. Former skipper Ephraim Longworth was one of the club's first legendary players and could play right and left full-back. He made his debut in September 1910 and stayed with the team until he was 40 years old in 1928. Longworth played 341 league games, and 370 in total, for the team and remarkably failed to score a single goal. He also failed to score in five outings for England, but did captain his homeland. Longworth did manage to score a few goals in war-time contests for Liverpool, but they aren't included in his official statistics.

9. When it comes to club records, these are all current as of September 15, 2020. Liverpool's biggest win was 11-0 in 1974 over Strømsgodset in the European Cup Winners' Cup. Their record league victory was 10-1 in 1899 when they beat Rotherham Town in a Second Division clash. The greatest FA Cup victory came in 1889 when they smashed Newtown 9-0 in second qualifying round action, and the club's top League Cup conquest was a 10-0 thrashing of Fulham in a second round, first-leg fixture in 1964.

10. Of course, Liverpool has also been on the wrong end of some beatings, and these are currently the club's record defeats. Their biggest ever loss was 9-1 at the hands of Birmingham City in a Second Division showdown in 1954. Their biggest home embarrassment was 6-0 to Sunderland in a First Division outing in 1930. The team's greatest FA Cup loss was 5-0 to the Bolton Wanderers in a fourth round, first-leg match in 1946, and they were also downed 5-0 in their record League Cup beating when Aston Villa blanked them 5-0 in the quarterfinals in 2019.

CHAPTER 10:

DOMESTIC COMPETITION

QUIZ TIME!

1. How many times has Liverpool shared the Charity/ Community Shield?

    a. 5

    b. 3

    c. 7

    d. 6

2. As of 2020, how many times has Liverpool won the top-flight league title?

    a. 17

    b. 18

    c. 19

    d. 20

3. Liverpool were the last recipients of the Sheriff of London Charity Shield in 1907.

    a. True

    b. False

4. Who did Liverpool defeat to win their first FA Cup?

    a. Fulham

    b. Leeds United

    c. Manchester United

    d. Sheffield Wednesday

5. When did the club win its first League Cup?

    a. 1979-80

    b. 1981-82

    c. 1978-79

    d. 1980-81

6. Who did Liverpool face in the 2001 FA Cup Final?

    a. Tottenham Hotspur

    b. Aston Villa

    c. Chelsea

    d. Arsenal

7. Liverpool defeated which club 2-1 to win their first League Cup?

    a. Watford

    b. Coventry City

    c. West Ham United

    d. Manchester City

8. Between 1979 and 1991, Liverpool won the league title seven times.

    a. True

    b. False

9. How many times has Liverpool won the Charity/Community Shield outright?

    a. 8

    b. 9

    c. 10

    d. 11

10. Which club did Liverpool defeat to win the Sheriff of London Charity Shield?

    a. Bury F.C.

    b. Corinthian F.C.

    c. Sheffield United

    d. Queens Park Rangers

11. Liverpool are the only winners of the Football League Super Cup.

    a. True

    b. False

12. In the 2012 League Cup Final, Liverpool faced which Second Division club?

    a. Cardiff City

    b. Southampton F.C.

    c. Burnley F.C.

    d. Crystal Palace

13. How many domestic doubles has Liverpool won as of 2020?

    a. 2

    b. 1

c. 4

d. 3

14. The Reds won the Second Division league title five times.

    a. True

    b. False

15. Who did Liverpool NOT play in the Football Super League Cup leading up to the Final?

    a. Norwich City

    b. Everton

    c. Tottenham Hotspur

    d. Southampton

16. Which team did the club meet in the fourth round of the 1995 League Cup?

    a. Blackburn Rovers

    b. Stoke City

    c. Ipswich Town

    d. Burnley F.C.

17. When did Liverpool win their first league title?

    a. 1889-90

    b. 1905-06

    c. 1900-01

    d. 1901-02

18. How many FA Cup titles has Liverpool won as of 2020?

    a. 6

    b. 8

c. 7

d. 9

19. How many League Cups has Liverpool won as of 2020?

    a. 3

    b. 5

    c. 8

    d. 9

20. The Reds currently hold the record for most English League Cup titles.

    a. True

    b. False

QUIZ ANSWERS

1. A – 5

2. C – 19

3. B – False

4. B – Leeds United

5. D – 1980-81

6. D – Arsenal

7. C – West Ham United

8. A – True

9. C – 10

10. B – Corinthian F.C.

11. A – True

12. A – Cardiff City

13. D – 3

14. B – False

15. B – Everton

16. A – Blackburn Rovers

17. C – 1900-01

18. C – 7

19. C – 8

20. A –True

DID YOU KNOW?

1. Liverpool has won 19 top-flight league titles throughout club history up to 2020, which is currently second to Manchester United's record of 20. This includes one in the Premier League, which launched in 1992-93, and 18 in the former First Division. The squad won crowns in the following campaigns: 1900-01, 1905-06, 1921-22, 1922-23, 1946-47, 1963-64, 1965-66, 1972-73, 1975-76, 1976-77, 1978-79, 1979-80, 1981-82, 1982-83, 1983-84, 1985-86, 1987-88, 1989-90, and 2019-20. The club also won the Second Division title in 1893-94, 1895-96, 1904-05, and 1961-62 for a total of 23 league championships.

2. The FA Cup has been won by Liverpool on seven occasions with the victories coming in: 1964-65, 1973-74, 1985-86, 1988-89, 1991-92, 2000-01, and 2005-06. In addition, The Reds currently hold the English record for Football League (EFL) Cup triumphs with eight. These were captured in: 1980-81, 1981-82, 1982-83, 1983-84, 1994-95, 2000-01, 2002-03, and 2011-12.

3. The FA Community Shield, formerly the FA Charity Shield, traditionally kicks off the English season with the FA Cup holders playing the winners of the Premier League (former First Division). Liverpool has won the trophy outright 10 times and has shared it another 5 times when the contest ended in a draw, for a total of 15. Their

outright wins came in: 1966, 1974, 1976, 1979, 1980, 1982, 1988, 1989, 2001, and 2006, with the title being shared in: 1964, 1965, 1977, 1986, and 1990.

4. The Sheriff of London Charity Shield was an annual competition, which was also known as the Dewar Shield. It was a contest pitting England's top professional team against the top amateur squad. The professional club was either the FA Cup or Football League champion from the previous year, while Corinthian usually represented the amateur club. The inaugural contest took place in 1898, with proceeds going to hospitals and charities, and it later became known as the FA Charity Shield. Currently, it is known as the FA Community Shield. Liverpool won the silverware in 1906 with a 5-2 conquest over Corinthian.

5. The Football League Super Cup took place just once, in 1985-86, and was also known as the ScreenSport Super Cup. It was operated by the English Football League as a way of raising money and providing competition to teams which had qualified for European tournaments the previous year but were banned from playing after by UEFA, as a result of the infamous Heysel Stadium disaster. It generated little interest from the clubs involved and was abolished after just one campaign. Liverpool won the tournament by beating Everton 7-2 on aggregate over two legs in the Final.

6. When Second Division titles are included, Liverpool had won a total of 55 domestic trophies/titles as of September 2020. Not included, though, is the Lancashire League,

which was the club's first ever piece of silverware in 1892-93. The first Football League title came in 1893-94 when they won the Second Division, and the first top-flight title was won in 1900-01 with the latest coming in 2019-20. The Reds first won the FA Cup in 1965 and the League Cup in 1981. The team's most successful decade came in the 1980s, when they captured six League championships, five Charity Shields, four League Cups, two European Cups, two FA Cups, and the Football League Super Cup.

7. The Hillsborough disaster occurred April 15, 1989, when Liverpool and Nottingham Forest met in an FA Cup semifinal at Hillsborough Stadium in Sheffield, the home ground of the Sheffield Wednesday football club. Liverpool fans in two standing-only sections were crushed by others trying to enter the stadium shortly before the match kicked off, resulting in the deaths of 96 people with another 766 injured. Sadly, it's the worst loss of life in British sports history, and it led to the introduction of all-seat stadiums in the top two flights of English football.

8. Although Liverpool have won seven FA Cups, they have also lost seven FA Cup Finals. Their biggest Final win came in 1974 when they downed Newcastle United 3-0 at Wembley Stadium in London. Their biggest final defeat was 2-0 at the hands of Arsenal in 1950 at Wembley. In addition, The Reds' Ian Rush currently holds the record for most goals scored in FA Cup Final games with five. The club has won one League and FA Cup double, which came in 1985-86.

9. When it comes to the English League Cup, Liverpool currently holds the record for most Cup wins at eight, most consecutive victories with four, and most appearances at 12. They share the records for biggest win in a match at 10-0 over Fulham and the biggest 11-goal aggregate win over two legs, with 13-2 over Fulham and 11-0 over Exeter City. The Reds' Ian Rush co-holds the record for most Final wins at five, most Finals appearances with six, and most goals in the competition with 50, while John Arne Riise scored the fastest goal in a Final after just 45 seconds in 2005. Liverpool has won two League and League Cup doubles, in 1981-82 and 1982-83.

10. For all of Liverpool's successful Cup runs over the years, they've also suffered some humiliating defeats at the hands of lower-level teams. One of these came for manager Roy Hodgson and his squad against Northampton in the third round of the 2010-11 League Cup at Anfield of all places. The fourth-tier team erased an early deficit for a 1-1 draw after 90 minutes. Northampton then took the lead in extra time with Liverpool equalizing with just four minutes to go. However, Northampton completed the upset by winning the penalty shootout 4-2.

CHAPTER 11:

EUROPE & BEYOND

QUIZ TIME!

1. In 2000-01, Liverpool won which international title for the club's second-ever treble?

    a. European Super Cup

    b. FIFA Club World Cup

    c. Champions League

    d. UEFA Cup

2. When did Liverpool win their first FIFA Club World Cup?

    a. 2007

    b. 2019

    c. 2005

    d. 2018

3. The first international title the club won was the European Cup in 1976-77.

    a. True

    b. False

4. How many times has Liverpool won the UEFA Cup as of 2020?

   a. 2

   b. 5

   c. 3

   d. 6

5. Liverpool faced which team in the 1977 European Cup Final?

   a. Borussia Mönchengladbach

   b. F.C. Zürich

   c. Dynamo Kyiv

   d. Club Brugge KV

6. Which club did Liverpool NOT play on their way to the 1978 European Cup Final?

   a. Benfica

   b. Dynamo Dresden

   c. Borussia Mönchengladbach

   d. Atlético Madrid

7. What was the final score in the 2005 European Super Cup Final victory against CSKA Moscow?

   a. 3-2

   b. 2-0

   c. 1-0

   d. 3-1

8. As of 2020, Liverpool has won 17 international titles.

   a. True

   b. False

9. Which fellow Premier League club did Liverpool defeat 5-4 in penalties to win the 2019 European Super Cup?

    a. Manchester United
    b. Tottenham Hotspur
    c. Chelsea
    d. Manchester City

10. Liverpool defeated which Bundesliga team to win the club's first European Super Cup in 1977?

    a. Hamburger SV
    b. F.C. Köln
    c. Bayern Munich
    d. Borussia Dortmund

11. Liverpool has completed three doubles with at least one international title.

    a. True
    b. False

12. How many times has Liverpool won the European Super Cup as of 2020?

    a. 7
    b. 2
    c. 5
    d. 4

13. Which year did Liverpool finish runner-up in the FIFA Club World Cup?

    a. 2000
    b. 2005

c. 2010

d. 2015

14. Liverpool is the first British club to win an international treble.

    a. True

    b. False

15. Who did Liverpool beat in the 2018-19 European Champions League Final?

    a. Juventus

    b. Ajax

    c. Tottenham Hotspur

    d. F.C. Barcelona

16. What was the final aggregate score for Liverpool in the 1977 European Super Cup?

    a. 3-0

    b. 7-1

    c. 4-2

    d. 6-0

17. Which Italian club did Liverpool beat in the 2004-05 Champions League Final?

    a. Inter Milan

    b. Roma

    c. AC Milan

    d. Juventus

18. Which club did Liverpool NOT play against in the 1973 UEFA Cup?

a. Eintracht Frankfurt

b. AEK F.C.

c. BFC Dynamo

d. Real Madrid

19. How many times have Liverpool won the European Cup/Champions League as of 2020?

a. 9

b. 7

c. 4

d. 6

20. Liverpool defeated Barcelona to win their first FIFA Club World Cup.

a. True

b. False

QUIZ ANSWERS

1. D – UEFA Cup

2. B – 2019

3. B – False

4. C – 3

5. A – Borussia Mönchengladbach

6. D – Atlético Madrid

7. D – 3-1

8. B – False

9. C – Chelsea

10. A – Hamburger SV

11. A – True

12. D – 4

13. B – 2005

14. A – True

15. C – Tottenham Hotspur

16. B – 7-1

17. C – AC Milan

18. D – Real Madrid

19. D – 6

20. B – False

DID YOU KNOW?

1. Liverpool is currently the most successful British club in international football with their haul of 14 trophies. This includes six European Cup/UEFA Champions League titles (1976-77, 1977-78, 1980-81, 1983-84, 2004-05, 2018-19), four European/UEFA Super Cups (1977, 2001, 2005, 2019), three UEFA Cups (1972-73, 1975-76, 2000-01), and a FIFA Club World Cup (2019). In addition, The Reds became the first English team to win the international treble of Champions League, Club World Cup, UEFA Super Cup.

2. The FIFA Club World Cup is operated by FIFA, has been in existence since 2000 and has been hosted by several different nations. In 2005, the FIFA Club World Championship merged with the Intercontinental Cup and renamed the FIFA Club World Cup a year later. The tournament features winners of various global competitions including the UEFA Champions League holders. Liverpool became just the second British and English winners in 2019, with a 1-0 win over Flamengo of Brazil in Qatar.

3. The Reds have won several doubles and trebles, which included a European title in them. They captured the English First Division and the European Cup in 1976-77; the English First Division and UEFA Cup in both 1972-73 and 1975-76; the English League Cup and the European Cup in 1980-81; the English First Division, the English

League Cup, and the European Cup in 1983-84; and the English FA Cup, English League Cup, and the UEFA Cup in 2000-01.

4. The Heysel Stadium disaster took place on May 29, 1985, at the European Cup Final between Liverpool and Juventus in Brussels, Belgium. Fans began fighting before the kickoff, and 39 of them died when a concrete retaining wall collapsed with approximately another 600 being injured. The game was still played with Juventus winning 1-0, and the incident led to all English football clubs being banned from all European competitions by UEFA until 1990, with Liverpool's ban lasting an extra year.

5. The club achieved a treble in 1983-84 when it topped the English First Division and captured the English League Cup and the European Cup. The league championship was the second of four consecutive as they beat runners-up Southampton by three points. The League Cup triumph was a Merseyside Derby, which ended in a 0-0 draw with Everton at Wembley. The Reds took the replay 1-0 at Maine Road in Manchester three days later. The team then won its fourth European crown by edging Roma 2-1 in a penalty shootout. Their 2000-01 campaign wasn't too shabby either as they took home the UEFA Cup along with the FA and League Cups.

6. One of the most controversial moments in Liverpool's European ventures took place at Anfield against Chelsea in the second leg of the 2005 semifinals. The Reds' Luis

García was awarded a goal shortly after kickoff to give the home side a 1-0 aggregate lead after the first leg ended 0-0. However, Chelsea argued that defender William Gallas cleared the ball off the goal line before it had a chance to fully cross it. Since there was no goal line technology back then, referee Lubos Michel had the final say and awarded the goal. Chelsea boss Jose Mourinho labeled it the "ghost goal," and it turned out to be the only one of the match.

7. Former skipper Steven Gerrard often scored dramatic goals for the club, and one of the most famous came in December 2004 at home against Olympiakos in the group stage of the European Champions League. The Reds needed to win by a pair of goals to advance to the knockout stage, but led only 2-1, with just four minutes remaining after fighting back from a 1-0 deficit. Gerrard got hold of the ball and smashed a tremendous long-range half-volley into the back of the net to guarantee his squad advanced with a 3-1 triumph. Naturally, Gerrard went to the Kop end of Anfield to celebrate and was then booked and suspended for the following match due to his exuberance.

8. Once again, Steven Gerrard was the catalyst for another famous Liverpool victory in the 2004-05 European Champions League with his heroics. This time, coming in the Final against AC Milan in Istanbul, Turkey. The Reds got off to a brutal start and trailed 3-0 at half-time, and some of their fans actually left the stadium. That was a mistake; Gerrard grabbed the match by the scruff of the neck as Liverpool leveled the score with three goals

between the 54th and 60th minutes. Gerrard scored the first and was brought down in the penalty box for the equalizer by Xabi Alonso on the rebound of the ensuing penalty. The Reds then won 3-2 in a penalty shootout.

9. Another huge difference maker in the 2004-05 European Champions League Final win over AC Milan was goalkeeper Jerzy Dudek. He more than pulled his weight by keeping Milan at bay with some sensational saves to make sure the Italian side never scored a fourth goal after 90 and 120 minutes of drama. During the penalty shootout, Dudek managed to distract Milan penalty takers with a rubber-leg routine and then saved a pair of spot kicks while his teammates took the shootout 3-2. The contest has often been called the most exciting Champions League Final ever.

10. One of the most recent epic comebacks by Liverpool took place in the 2018-19 European Champions League semifinals at Anfield. They dropped the first leg 3-0 in Spain to La Liga champions Barcelona but managed to defy all odds by edging Lionel Messi and his squad 4-3 in the second leg. Divock Origi opened the scoring in the seventh minute with Georginio Wijnaldum, then scoring twice within 122 seconds, just 10 minutes into the second half. The miracle comeback was then completed when Origi made it 4-0 with 11 minutes to go, and The Reds would go on to beat Tottenham Hotspur 2-0 in the Final.

CHAPTER 12:

TOP SCORERS

QUIZ TIME!

1. Who scored five goals in a game against the Fleetwood Rangers in 1892-93?

   a. Tom Wyllie

   b. John Miller

   c. Malcolm McVean

   d. John Smith

2. Which player was the first Liverpool player to win the scoring title in 1902-03?

   a. Robbie Robinson

   b. George Allan

   c. Jack Parkinson

   d. Sam Raybould

3. Sam Raybould scored 27 goals in 1902-03.

   a. True

   b. False

4. Which player has scored the most goals across all competitions in a season as of 2020?

   a. Robbie Fowler
   b. Mohamed Salah
   c. Ian Rush
   d. Roger Hunt

5. Who led the team in goals in 1987-88?

   a. Ronnie Whelan
   b. Paul Walsh
   c. John Aldridge
   d. Alan Irvine

6. How many goals did Ian Rush score in 65 appearances in 1983-84?

   a. 47
   b. 31
   c. 40
   d. 45

7. Who was the club's leading scorer across all competitions in 2016-17?

   a. Roberto Firmino
   b. Sadio Mané
   c. Divock Origi
   d. Philippe Coutinho

8. Luis Suárez won the team scoring title in 2013-14 with 30 goals.

   a. True
   b. False

9. Roger Hunt led The Reds in scoring with how many league goals in 1965-66?

  a. 28
  b. 29
  c. 30
  d. 31

10. How many seasons did Jimmy Melia lead the squad in league goals?

  a. 1
  b. 3
  c. 2
  d. 4

11. Michael Owen led the club in scoring in all competitions for seven straight seasons.

  a. True
  b. False

12. Who scored 33 goals across all competitions in 2007-08?

  a. Peter Crouch
  b. Fernando Torres
  c. Dirk Kuyt
  d. Yossi Benayoun

13. Which player has scored the most goals as a substitute for Liverpool?

  a. Daniel Sturridge
  b. David Fairclough
  c. Ryan Babel
  d. Steven Gerrard

14. Mohamed Salah and Sadio Mané each had 22 league goals in 2018-19.

    a. True
    b. False

15. How many goals did David Fairclough score as a substitute for Liverpool?

    a. 17
    b. 15
    c. 23
    d. 18

16. In 2004-05, which of these players didn't score 13 goals in all competitions?

    a. Steven Gerrard
    b. Luis García
    c. John Arne Riise
    d. Milan Baroš

17. As of 2020, how many different Liverpool players have won/shared a Premier League Golden Boot award?

    a. 4
    b. 10
    c. 6
    d. 9

18. Who led the club with 36 goals in 1995-96?

    a. Neil Ruddock
    b. Stan Collymore
    c. Steve McManaman
    d. Robbie Fowler

19. How many Premier League Golden Boot titles have Liverpool players won/shared as of 2020?

    a. 4

    b. 8

    c. 5

    d. 10

20. In 1903-04, Jack Cox was the club's leading scorer in league action with nine goals.

    a. True

    b. False

QUIZ ANSWERS

1. B – John Miller

2. D – Sam Raybould

3. B – False

4. C – Ian Rush

5. C – John Aldridge

6. A – 47

7. D – Philippe Coutinho

8. B – False

9. B – 29

10. A – 1

11. A – True

12. B – Fernando Torres

13. B – David Fairclough

14. A – True

15. D – 18

16. C – John Arne Riise

17. A – 4

18. D – Robbie Fowler

19. C – 5

20. A – True

DID YOU KNOW?

1. Roger Hunt is the current top scorer in league games for the club with 244 of them under his belt in 404 contests. Hunt also notched 285 markers in 492 outings in all competitions between 1959 and 1969. He won two First Division titles with the team and an FA Cup as well as a Second Division title. Known as "Sir Roger" by Liverpool supporters, Hunt was also a member of the England squad that hoisted the 1966 World Cup at Wembley with three goals in the tournament. The forward scored a club-record 41 league goals in the 1961-62 season and a record five hat tricks in the campaign.

2. The top scorer in all competitions for Liverpool is currently Ian Rush as he deposited the ball into the net 346 times in 660 games, with 229 goals coming in 469 league outings. He also holds club records for most FA Cup and League Cup goals, most League Cup appearances, most goals in a season and is the top scorer in the Merseyside Derby with 25. The former Welsh international had two stints with The Reds from 1980-87 and 1988-96. He also tallied 28 goals for Wales in 73 appearances. He helped The Reds win five League titles, three FA Cups, five League Cups, and a European Cup.

3. Former Scottish international Kenny Dalglish is another Liverpool legend as a player for and manager of the club

and was also director of football. He posted 172 goals in 515 appearances with 118 goals in 355 league encounters. He also scored 167 times in 322 matches for Glasgow Celtic and notched 30 goals in a record 1-2 games for Scotland. He won several personal awards as a player and appeared for Liverpool between 1977 and 1990. Dalglish also managed The Reds between 1985 and 1991 and 2011-12. As a Liverpool player, he helped the team to six league titles, an FA Cup, four League Cups, three European Cups, and a European Super Cup.

4. Known as "Mighty Mouse" by fans, forward Kevin Keegan scored an even 100 goals for the club in 323 outings with 68 coming in 230 league matches. And even though he is just 5 feet 8 inches tall, he scored numerous times with his head and added another 21 markers for England in 63 contests. Keegan starred for Liverpool from 1971 to 1977 and won three First Division titles, two UEFA Cups, an FA Cup, and the European Cup. He left The Reds for Hamburger SV in Germany and was named European Footballer of the Year in 1978 and 1979. Keegan later managed several top-flight teams as well as the English national side.

5. South African-born Gordon Hodgson often scored in bunches as he currently holds the club records for career hat tricks with 17. He also owns the team mark for most league goals in a top-flight season with 36 in 40 games in 1930-31. Hodgson suited up for Liverpool between 1926 and 1935 and banged in 241 goals in 377 clashes, with 233

of those coming in 358 league ventures. The forward played briefly for the South African and English national teams, was a top-class cricket player, and entered management when retiring as a player.

6. As of September 2020, Liverpool's youngest ever goalscorer has been Ben Woodburn. He was just 17 years and 45 days of age when he tallied against Leeds United in a League Cup clash on November 29, 2016. The oldest to score so far was Scottish international Billy Liddell on March 5, 1960, when he found the net against Stoke City at the age of 38 years and 55 days. Woodburn is a Welsh international who turns 20 years old in October 2021, while Liddell is presently the club's fourth leading all-time scorer with 228 goals in 534 games between 1946 and 1960. He also led the team in scoring eight different seasons.

7. Even though Harry (Henry) Chambers signed for Liverpool in 1915, the forward had to wait until 1919 to begin his Anfield career due to World War I. He played 339 times for the club until 1928 and contributed 151 goals in 339 contests, with 135 league goals in 310 outings. He also managed five goals in eight ventures with England. After scoring on his Reds debut, Chambers, who was nicknamed "Smiler," led the squad in scoring for the following five seasons and helped the side win two First Division titles.

8. Sam Raybould scored 10 times in 13 league matches for non-league club New Brighton, and manager Tom Watson

signed him for The Reds in January 1900. The striker scored a then-record 31 league goals in 1902-03 and totaled 130 goals in 226 games until 1907, with 120 league goals in 211 contests. When he retired, he remained the team's top career scorer for 37 years, and his 67 goals in his first 100 games for the squad was a record until Mohamed Salah broke it in 2020.

9. As of September 2020, the top 20 career goalscorers in all competitions for Liverpool were: Ian Rush 346, Roger Hunt 285, Gordon Hodgson 241, Billy Liddell 228, Steven Gerrard 186, Robbie Fowler 183, Kenny Dalglish 172, Michael Owen 158, Harry Chambers 151, Sam Raybould 130, Jack Parkinson 128, Dick Forshaw 123, Ian St John 118, Jack Balmer 110, John Barnes 108, Kevin Keegan 100, Mohamed Salah 97, John Toshack 96, Albert Stubbins 83, and Luis Suárez 82. It should be noted that Mohamed Salah was still playing with the club as of September 2020.

10. When it comes to goals-per-game ratio, these are the top 20 former Liverpool scorers who appeared in at least 100 games with the club: Gordon Hodgson (.639), Luis Suárez (.617), John Aldridge (.606), Jack Parkinson (.584), Roger Hunt (.579), Sam Raybould (.575), Fernando Torres (.570), Michael Owen (.532), Ian Rush (.524), Robbie Fowler (.496), John Evans (.495), Albert Stubbins (.466), Joe Hewitt (.451), Harry Chambers (.445), Dick Forshaw (.427), Billy Liddell (.427), Daniel Sturridge (.419), John Wark (.389), John Toshack (.389), and Tom Miller (.384).

CONCLUSION

Being turned down by the English Football League as Everton Athletic, England's newest club in 1892 was then christened Liverpool F.C., and the rest, as they say, is history.

"The Reds" went undefeated in their first year in the Football League to win the Second Division, and it was just a sign of things to come. The team has continued to thrill and entertain supporters across the world for over 125 years with their never-say-die attitude and were crowned Premier League champions as recently as 2019-20.

Liverpool has won over five dozen pieces of silverware over the years with domestic league titles, FA Cups, League Cups, Charity/Community Shields, and numerous European Cups. They're currently one of the toughest teams in the world to beat, and even more trophies could soon be on the way to Anfield.

The trivia/fact book you've just looked through re-lives the club's famous history every step of the way right until the kickoff of the 2020-21 Premier League campaign.

There's an endless array of lighthearted trivia questions and facts inside these pages, along with 120 short anecdotes regarding the club, its players and managers, etc. This includes the club's 30-year drought in winning a top-flight league title and the unfortunate, tragic incidents in the European Cup and FA Cup.

We trust you enjoyed reading it as much as we did writing it, and hopefully, you'll be able to use the book when preparing for your next big Liverpool F.C. trivia battle.

Liverpool supporters are extremely loyal and always stand by their team through thick and thin. Thanks for being one of them and taking the time to read the latest Reds trivia/fact book.

Made in the USA
Monee, IL
19 June 2022

98282851R00075